POETRY IN MOTION
THE BIRTH OF SUCCESS II

POETIC ANTHOLOGIES
Featuring:
Kelly Miller Middle School
H.D. Woodson SYEP 2014 &
Lincoln Heights Book-In-A-Week Program

**POETRY BY
DO THE WRITE THING YOUTH OF DC**

Written and published by students participating in a program sponsored by
Do The Write Thing Foundation of DC

© Copyright 2014 by each individual author

All Rights Reserved. No part of this book may be reproduced or transmitted in any form or by any means electronic or mechanical, including photocopying, recording or by an information storage or retrieval system, except by a reviewer who may quote brief passages in a review to be printed in a magazine or by a newspaper, without the permission of the publisher.

Design © 2014 Gloria Marconi Illustration & Design

Edited by Marion D. Ingram

Printed in the United States of America
ISBN: 978-1-50-23644-94

Published by Do The Write Thing of DC
Washington, DC 20001

www.dothewritething1@gmail.com
www.dothewritinginc.org

POETRY IN MOTION

CONTENTS

Acknowledgements | 5
About the Programs | Staff | 6
Foreword: Marion Ingram | 7

KELLY MILLER POETRY CLUB
My Life | 11
   Jasmine Jones 13
   Tabriya Hull 14
   Ariana Gatlin 15
   Dashawn Robinson 16
   Daquan Horton 16
   Mikayla Riggs 17
   Iyana Thompson 17
   Malik Satterwhite-Austin 18
   Chardonae Zimmerman 18

Where I'm From | 21
   Chantese Zimmerman 23
   Breona Meniefield 23
   Ariana Gatlin 24
   Jasmine Jones 24
   Messiah Tourf 25
   Iyana Thompson 26

Free Verse | 27
   L'Nyah Wright 29
   Jasmine Jones 30
   Daquan Horton 30
   Jessica Parks 31
   Breneah Sprilill 32
   Iyana Thompson 33
   Makiyah Steele 34
   Jessica Parks 35
   Jasmine Jones 35
   Ariel Proctor 36
   Daquan Horton 36
   I'Nyah Wright 38
   Jasmine Jones 39
   Julia Ellington 40
   Tabriya Hull 40

   Schniya Stallings 41
   Iyana Thompson 42
   Daquan Horton 43

Clerihews | 45
   Ariel Proctor 47
   Messiah Tourf 47
   Iyana Thompson 47
   Ariana Gatlin 47
   Ariana Gatlin 48
   Breona Meniefield 48
   Daquan Horton 48

Haiku | 49
   Daquan Horton 51
   Charity Chakwa 51
   Breona Meniefield 51
   Jasmine Jones 52
   L'Nyah Wright 52
   Rashad Young 52
   Tony Hopkins 53
   Iyana Thompson 53
   Ariana Gatlin 53

H.D. WOODSON SYEP | 55
Anti Bullying Campaign | 57
Introduction | 58
   Timothy Bey 59
   Aziza Withers 60-61
   Keonte Townsend 62
   George Anderson 62
   Damoni Tolson 63
   Mic'Quon Contee 63
   Joseph Hailey 64
   Keonte Townsend 64
   Charnisha Brown 65
   Sydney Mckenzie 65
   Tymia Bailey 66
   Toni Hawkins 66
   Amony Johnson 67
   Paprika Berry 67
   Christopher Tate 68
   Maurice Edwards 68

4 THE BIRTH OF SUCCESS

Terin Collins **64**
Nya Morton **69**
Kyndall Jones **70**
Keva Iracks **71**
Andre Amalemba **71**
Daschmiere Fenwick **72**
Aisha Ferguson **73**
Destiny Sanders **73**
MyKalyah Ware **74**
Jalon Rowe **75**
Tanika Garner **76**
Ciera Oliver **77**

Where I'm From | 81
Dajeh Johnson **83**
Charnisha Brown **83**
Tymia Bailey **84**
Unknown **84**
Asia Thorne **85**
D'Angelo Holley **85**
Jalon Rowe **86**
Aujanae Barnum **86**

Clerihews | 87
Charnisha Brown **89**
Nya Morton **90**
Rajae Jackson **90**
Dajeh Johnson **91**
Asia Thorne **91**
Modane Robinson **92**
Jailyn Sekou **92**
MyKalyah Ware **93**
Tymia Bailey **93**
Toni Hawkins **94**

Visual Haiku | 95
Charnisha Brown **97**
Unknown **97**
Tymia Bailey **98**
Asia Thorne **98**
Paprika Berry **99**
Daschmiere Fenwick **99**
Troy Williams **100**
Afia Tyus **100**

Free Verse/Short Stories | **101**
Makaylah Ware
103, 104, 105, 106, 107
Kyndall Jones **112**
Afia Tyus **113**
Toni Hawkins **115, 116**

LINCOLN HEIGHTS | 119

Anti-Bullying Poems | 121
Kiamonee Smith **123**
Chynna Dandridge **123**
Zyaja Cook **124**
Jonquil Hawkins **124**
Jasmia Hawkins **125**
Cortez Smith **125**
Alijah Gladden **127**
Willis Davon **128**
Taichelle Miller **128**
Chardonae Zimmerman **130**

Where I'm From | 131
Jasmia Hawkins **133**
Javonte Campbell **133**
Zyaja Cook **134**
Jonquil Hawkins **134**
Alijah Gladden **135**
Chynna Dandridge **135**
Secret Webb **136**

Haikus & Clerihews | 137
Jamel Hawkins **139**
Shmirah Horton **139**
Chyna Ann McLain **139**
Secret Webb **140**
Chynna Dandridge **140**
Keyon Webb **140**
Chardonae Zimmerman **141**
Kiamonee Smith **141**
Zyaja Cook **142**
Alijah Gladden **143**
Javonte Campbell **143**
Chynna Dandridge **144**

ACKNOWLEDGMENTS

This anthology represents the work of youth participating in three different programs: (1) 2013-2014 after-school Poetry Club at Kelly Miller Middle School, (2) Summer 2014 Book-In-A-Week program at Lincoln Heights Community Center and (3) 2014 SYEP at Woodson Senior High School.

First, we would like to thank Ms. Frenchie Davis, Coordinator of After-School Programs at Kelly Miller Middle School, for her assistance during the 2013-2014 school year. We would also like to thank Ms. Dorothy Dinkins, President, Resident Council at Lincoln Heights, for inviting us to work with youth residing in this public housing development.

We want to thank Mayor Vincent Gray for his continued leadership in maintaining and supporting the Summer Youth Employment Program and making it possible for District youth to participate in unique experiences while being compensated. Thanks also to DOES staff: F. Thomas Luparello, Director; Gerren Price, Deputy Director of Youth Programs; Thennie Freeman, Associate Director and Manager of Youth Programs; Kathy Guevara and Vanessa Weatherington, Program Coordinators. Additional thanks goes to the staff at H.D. Woodson High School, the site for our program, for providing space, nutritious meals, and security that maintained a safe and secure environment.

We also want to acknowledge Daniela Grigioni, Office of Out-of-School Time Programs, DC Public Schools, who was a major resource for us as she worked hard to secure Woodson SHS as our summer site.

Thank you also to those organizations that provided financial support for our programs: DC Children and Youth Investment Trust Corporation (Ed Davies, Executive Director); D.C. Commission on the Arts and Humanities (Lionell Thomas, Executive Director; Moshe Adams, Director of Grants), and the DC Department of Employment Services.

ABOUT THE PROGRAM

Do The *Write* Thing Foundation of DC (DTWT) was incorporated in the District of Columbia as a nonprofit corporation in 2010, and received its tax exempt 501(c)(3) that same year. This organization sponsors summer and after-school programs for youth, age 14–18. During the summers, DTWT serves as a site for the D.C. Department of Employment Services so participating youth get paid to participate in poetry writing/publishing, songwriting and video production.

These workshops result in the publication of a book of poems, production of songs in a mobile recording studio, and production of videos.

2014 SYEP STAFF

Marion D. Ingram, *Executive Director*
Carla A. Nordé, *Program Coordinator*
Braxton Dunmore, *Program Coordinator*

FOREWORD

This book contains poems from some of the nation's capital's most engaged youth. It was very rewarding as a mentor and instructor to involve these youth in a poetry writing workshop series so they could experience poetry from the inside out.

Do The Write Thing also provided youth opportunities to grow as writers of poetry and grow personally through authentic performance showcase. The youth were taught to recognize what makes a poem engaging and entertaining to a reader. In the process, our participants were able to heighten their confidence and develop critical discernment and self-expression skills.

The youth moved beyond the staid notions of what poetry is and discovered poetry as a treasure that brings light to language. The workshop series enhanced the students' understanding and appreciation of various forms of verse, particularly haiku, free verse and clerihew.

This collection also includes a campaign to end bullying. The aim is to inform, enthuse and inspire young people and school staff to address bullying in their schools during Anti-Bullying Week (Nov. 16-22, 2014) and beyond.

Marion Duane Ingram

M. Duane Ingram
Executive Director

8

10 THE BIRTH OF SUCCESS

12 THE BIRTH OF SUCCESS

MY LIFE POEM

Jasmine Jones

My Life
My life is like a garden that
Grows and grows because we grow
Each and every day

My life is like a paradise that
Helps me relax each day
Because of the way that my day
Had gone today

My life is like a riot each and
Every day because of the
Non sense that happens on my way

My life is like a celebration
That happens every day
Because when we hear music
We be dancing all the day

My life is like a magical journey
That I go on each and every night
But when I fall asleep my dream
Is pure and bright

MY LIFE POEM

Tabriya Hull

My sister is my life
Without her I would not breathe
I cannot live
If she is not with me
I don't know what to say
Except I would forever go away
If she is gone
I will go too.

I cannot think
What I would say
But
If she goes
I go the same way
My Life

MY LIFE POEM

Ariana Gatlin

My life is like a pile of apples
Some are sweet and some are sour.

My life is like a tree
I still can grow but if someone cuts
Me down I'm dead.

My life is like a volcano
I can erupt like tectonic plates
When I get mad.

My life is like a machine.
I can do anything I want as long
As I have that special something.

My life is like a stop sign.
I stop those who want to fight or harm me.

My life is like the floor.
You can step on me but you just can't break me.

MY LIFE POEM

Dashawn Robinson

My life is like an injured football player because I stay hurting myself.

My life is like a cheetah because I love to run.

My life is like a star because I shine bright.

My life is like a cloud because I am free.

My life is like a crying baby because it is so sad.

MY LIFE POEM

Daquan Horton

My life is like a tear
Brought in the world then taken out.

My life is like a ghost
None sees me as I want to be.

My life is like a nightmare
My mind won't think straight

My life is like school
I'm always learning.

My life is like a demon
People try to control but God strikes them down.

MY LIFE POEM

Mikayla Riggs

My life is like a haunted house because I fear people.

My life is like a fire because I get mad easily.

My life is like a diamond because I like to shine and stand out.

My life is like a star because I glow.

My life is like a heart because I show love to people.

MY LIFE POEM

Iyana Thompson

My life is like listening
To an indie rock band because
You can hear them fight for their
Life when the bass drops.

My life is like
Trying to finish a crossword puzzle
When you know they're no right answers
Because there's no right way to live.

My life is like going to New York
For the first time finally feeling alive.

My life is like a Taylor Swift song
Always having a hidden meaning.

My life is like the ending to Catching Fire
Because I don't know what's to come.

MY LIFE POEM

Malik Satterwhite–Austin

My life is like the playground because I stay playing.
My life is like a video game because I play it all day.
My life is like a winner because I stay winning.
My life is like candy because I like to eat it.
My life is like a light because I'm light as one.

MY LIFE POEM

Chardonae Zimmerman

My life is like a roller coaster because I go up and down.
My life is like the sun because I rise.
My life is like school because I like to learn.
My life is like music because I stay loud.
My life is respect because I respect others.

MY LIFE POEM

Marcellos Kosh–Mannin

My life is important.

My life is fun because I like to do fun things.

My life is helpful because I like to help people that need help.

In life I want to try my best because you can do anything you want in your life and today was a good day.

MY LIFE POEM

Chantese Zimmerman

My life is like a career because I know what I want to be.

My life is like the sun because I am so bright.

My life is like an empty coloring book that needs to be filled in.

My life is like a singer because I take stuff seriously.

My life is like school because I stay trying to learn.

MY LIFE POEM

Breona Menifield

My life is like a roller coaster because I have my ups and downs.
My life is like a shadow because I never make a sound.
My life is like a puppy because I'm always bouncing around.
My life is like fame because the paparazzi are trying
    to bring me down.
My life is like the sun because I'm always shining.

MY LIFE POEM

Ariel Proctor

My life is like a roller coaster going up and down.
My life is like a boring book which people choose to ignore.
My life is like a sponge because I have so much to absorb.
My life is like a shadow because I don't come out much.
My life is like a rule that people TRY to break.

COME TO WHERE I'M FROM

22 THE BIRTH OF SUCCESS

WHERE I'M FROM POEM

Chantese Zimmerman

Where I am from is like a game
People choose to play
Where I am from is like a playground
Full of kids ready to play
Where I am from is like a club where
People choose to be
Where I am from is like a neighborhood getting trashed
Where I am from is like a church
Full of people ready to shout

WHERE I'M FROM POEM

Breona Meniefield

Where I am from is the ghetto where hell breaks loose.
Where I am from is like a playground full of kids.
Where I am from I hear gunshots.
Where I am from is dangerous.
Where I am from is D.C.

WHERE I'M FROM POEM

Ariana Gatlin

Where I'm from people don't understand me like I want them to.

Where I'm from cars screech and beep and don't care if the people in the building can hear in their sleep.

Where I come from trees fall down just by the wind blowing so hard.

Where I come from storms are clues for people to shoot people from their windows.

WHERE I'M FROM POEM

Jasmine Jones

Where I'm from is where family can relax.

Where I'm from is a meadow full of flowers in a valley.

Where I'm from is where fights, and rights and riots start.

Where I'm from is where I just talk.

Where I'm from is a place that relaxes you.

WHERE I'M FROM POEM

Messiah Tourf

Where I'm from is not
Where I wanna be
Where I'm from
Nothing is ever free
Where I'm from
You think with your fists
Where I'm from
People don't have minds like this
Where I'm from
You have to figure out what's a lie
Shrivel and hide the world's too extreme
At this time
Where I'm from
You stick to the ignorance
Because being ignorant is always
Bliss.

WHERE I'M FROM POEM

Iyana Thompson

Where I'm from I'm looked at as weird.
An outsider that's getting ruined by the cause.
Where I'm from many don't take pride
Where I'm from people would rather go to jail than be a snitch.
They solve their problems with the ignorance of their fist.
Where I'm from is unknown to the human race.
Where I'm from my mind can't comprehend "Why?"
Where I'm from I want to be somewhere else.

Free Verse

Free Form

NO RULES

28 THE BIRTH OF SUCCESS

FRIENDS CAN BE ENEMIES

I'Nyah Wright

We are friends, we are enemies.
I'm me and you're you. If you're not me who are you?
I'm so much more than you.

You're mad at me for what?

Because I got a higher grade on my test and you didn't even pass? My world doesn't revolve around you. Is it because I'm courageous and you're carpooling? My world doesn't revolve around you.

You will never be much more than me. I'm higher than what you'll ever be. No matter how much you have tried I will still be the best.

We are enemies, I'm sad you're happy for what? Because I could've done better on my science test because I'm sad you have to be happy? Do you prey off peoples' sadness or when they're feeling down?

It seems like when I'm up you're down. When I'm down you're up and that's not fair. It's like you have nothing else better to do. The world doesn't revolve around you that's why we could never be just friends!

A MIDDLE SCHOOL LIFE IS FULL OF UPS AND DOWNS!

Jasmine Jones

A middle school life is full of ups and downs. When all things good turn into a frown. Good things have a cause and effect that always turns when you do something incorrect.

A middle school life is full of ups and downs. When you don't have friends to stick around. You're so shy since you're new to the school. Bullies will try to make you look like a fool.

DOUBT

Daquan Horton

Does life actually matter? People say God only made us live to die. We're bound to go to hell because the seven deadly sins cannot be avoided, thinking about condemns and yet you're born with it. You breathe from it, it's part of human nature, doubt reaches everywhere but not toward my Savior. Do you know the actual reason He saved you? Confused like the sun was wearing a blazer. Life is scary like hell raiser; I know why I'm here. Aren't you shocked like a Taser; I had no doubt about my Savior. He is real and fully loaded. To lose a clip of anointing and glory giving our clothes a sowing and now realize that the true you is worth showing. Now stop the doubt and get the devil's car towing.

DISRESPECT

Jessica Parks

Do you ever feel how people just treat you so rude and then you always want to say something back and you do! Yes I do because to me people like to express their own words. Some people like to speak their own mind and some people don't. To me people just like to speak their own words.

IT'S A FREE COUNTRY!

THE WAY SHE MAKES ME FEEL & THE WAY I MAKE HER FEEL.

Breneah Sprilill

The way I love my mom
Is like she has never been
Loved before.

She makes me feel
Like I'm the only girl
In the world.

I feel happy around her
My mom makes my day
She's the best.
I love her.

She is like a God
To me.
I respect her.
She makes me feel
Safe.

The way she loves me
Is like I've never been
Loved before.
I love her until death
Do us part.

That's why she's the best
And there's nothing no one
Can do about it.

UNTITLED

Iyana Thompson

He walked down the street hoping to be awakened from this demon in his head. Keeping him vacant like a banshee he screams for reality but only finding immortality. What happens when he figures out nothing good comes from having all these fantasies? What will happen when he's reaching the end of mortality?

How does he know that it is a nightmare if it's his reality? If he cuts, does that stop him from bleeding? When days don't get better does that mean they're repeating?

Well these questions were asked a little late.
The demons have now taken over his head.

I'M SMART

Makiyah Steele

I'm so fresh
I'm so clean
I'm so beautiful
And you so pitiful

I look like Nicki Minaj
And you look like
A ugly version of cupid.

Sorry!
I did it again.
I severed you.
You can't mess with this
Because I'm untouchable.

That's why I'm
Me and it's
Nothing you
Can do about it.

THE BLESSINGS ARE FALLING.

Jessica Parks

The blessings are falling
When God speaks to me.

The blessings are falling
When I hear Jesus calling me.

The blessings are falling
When I got saved for my lord and savior.

The blessings are falling
When I shout for joy.

The blessings are falling
When I look at myself and say
"God bless America"

FINALLY THE BLESSINGS ARE FALLING
EVERYWHERE IN OUR LIFE!

PEACE IS UNBROKEN

Jasmine Jones

I just don't care
For what you despair

So don't talk to me
Because I just don't care

So, leave me alone
'Cause I don't talk to you

So, I just don't care
So sad.

Bye to you!

OUR ANSWER BACK

Ariel Proctor

When we stare at the sky at night wondering when God is going to answer your prayers,

God already answered your prayer by blessing you and giving you talent.

So if you're ever wondering when he is going to answer back just remember how you wake up alive every morning.

THANKFUL

Ariel Proctor

Being thankful is the opposite of being ungrateful.

I thank God every day for letting me live.

I thank my mom for being there every step of the way.

I thank my family for protecting me.

I thank God for the angels he sent to watch over me.

I am thankful for everything you do for me.

TRATO UNJUSTO MARRISA, ALEXANDER, TRAVON MARTIN, JORDAN DAVIS

Daquan Horton

What do they have in common?

All have just been punished for being Black. They didn't have a chance to fight back. Protecting herself, Marrisa got 20 years in prison harming no one, firing a warning shot. Travon was just walking in the wrong spot. The suspect shot him that's a fact. Yet he didn't see the prison bars. Michael Denn killing black teens having fun and hiding from the crowds killed Jordan Davis for playing music too loud. What does that tell me growing up as a child? I'm scared to love and scared to die. It's still hard for Blacks, but I want to believe and strive to achieve to relieve the thoughts of to leave this earth behind. To never again breathe and with those eyes God they may see. We can succeed, all we need is to strike back economy. Let's expand our minds, get well educated, gain careers, and let things go, shed no tears, and show no fear. It's Black History Month, so our time starts here. Release that African Beast that was once on a leash but NOW CAN'T ADMIT DEFEAT.

I'M THE HERO WHO'S SAVING THE HERO ALL ALONG!

I'Nyah Wright

When I'm in trouble
You're my hero
When I've fallen and can't get up
You're my hero

When I'm stuck in a hole
And can't get out and you're not
My hero I start to lose hope
You showed me that I'm my own hero.

When someone's being bullied
And needs help I'm their hero
When they've fallen and can't get up
In their hero

At least when it's me being the hero
I don't give up I keep trying.
I help the people who want and need
To be helped and I make sure they don't
Lose hope.

Why?
Because I'm the hero who's
Saving the people who needs
The hero's help.

This time I thought you were saving me
And then it was me being our hero
All along.

Why can't we be our own hero?
At least if we all are heroes
There would be less trouble
Then how can we all
Be heroes if there's
No crime to fight
Then we would just be ordinary people.
So should there
Be more heroes or
Should it just be me?

I'm The HERO Who's Saving the HERO All Along!

TEN THINGS THAT I WANT TO SAY TO A CHILD THAT'S AFRAID OF ALL TYPES OF THINGS:

Jasmine Jones

1. Don't be afraid of bullies; Stand up for yourself and go tell an adult.
2. Don't be afraid of the dark it's just objects' shadows and have a night light by your side.
3. Don't be afraid of thunder it might be scary at first just keep away from the windows.
4. Don't be afraid of being wrong in class. Just try your best to answer the questions.
5. Don't be afraid of a dog. Just make sure you stay away from a dog that bites and make sure you have an adult.
6. Don't be afraid of a cat. Just try to stay away from their claws and their teeth.
7. Don't be afraid of challenges. Just work hard at them.
8. Don't be afraid of dancing. Dance your own dance. Don't worry about what other people say about your dancing.
9. Don't be afraid to encourage yourself about dancing, reading, or whatever you do.
10. Be yourself and stay away from all the animals.

THINGS I WILL WANT TO SAY TO MY SISTER!

Julia Ellington

The way you treat me, the way I feel when you ignore me. The way my heart broke. The way you love me is the way you don't but I still love you like one of my own even though we fight and even though we argue but I still love you like I should. The way you love me is the way I treat you but I still love you like my own.

UNTITLED

Tabriya Hull

Gun violence is wrong
I don't agree
When the cats are stuck in the tree
You see bad people on the streets

Why was it created?
Who would dare?
Look into the world with a gloomy glare.

I don't understand where we live
Gun violence is in the air
Just let it go far away

MOTHER LOVE

Schniya Stallings

My mother is someone I can't replace
Because she's the one who
Would be there with
Me no matter the race
Or who's chasing me with
Disgrace

My mother is passion
Without the depression
I love her no matter
What reaction we laugh
We play and we also converse
My mother is a lover
Gives me hugs with a
Thought of love

PRIZED POSSESSION
Iyana Thompson

Music is the one thing that keeps me
Through the day.
I listen to it whenever I can.
The genres are different
Emotions that I feel
It's my life with lyrics
Eminem are for when I am
Feeling mad or sad and have know
Where to go. When my father died
It kept me through the day.
Pop music cheers me up.
When music rushes through my veins
I gain an adrenaline rush.

PRIZED POSSESSION
Daquan Horton

My prized possessions you shouldn't take, if I don't have a mind I'll be confused of expression.
The poems I write are lessons and feelings through my life I developed and life has just sped up.
My soul isn't in an auction so I'll never put it up.
Education I developed from friends and family growing up.
See death is sad but it can't get to my heart or love.
God watches over above, my religion I couldn't ever give up.
Because it's something I love.
Sometimes my friends are stuck up.
My family gives me really tough love.
Even though life is rough and is a person that pushes and shoves
Not only physically, verbally and mentally pissing me off.
Taking my identity, so I can't remember me.
Attending life visually in my poems asking God for answers please.

44 THE BIRTH OF SUCCESS

Cler
i
hews

46 THE BIRTH OF SUCCESS

Miley Cyrus

Has no stylist
Always twerking instead of working

　　–Ariel Proctor

Taylor Swift

Yeah she's really fast
Runs through boy friends
Like she's running track

　　–Messiah T

Taylor Swift

Has many number one hits
But if I weren't her exes
She wouldn't be the nexus

　　–Iyana Thompson

Justin Bieber

Just another true diva
He says he's confident
But in reality he lost his evidence

–Iyana Thompson

Justin Bieber

I don't have no fever
He went with Selena
Also with Catrina

　　–Ariana Gatlin

THE BIRTH OF SUCCESS

Drake is not good
He didn't understood
Eminem said don't be a retard
He meant that he doesn't even go hard

—Ariana Gatlin

Drake got fame
But he is lame
He has no game

—Breona Meniefield

Drake wrote a song
About headlines
When he has
No headline

—Breona Meniefield

Carmelo Anthony

Does things for vanity
On the he bleed
Then he would take head

—Daquan Horton

Serena Williams

Seen someone on her bed
She wanted to kill them
Used her racket instead

—Daquan Horton

俳句

haiku

50 THE BIRTH OF SUCCESS

POETRY IN MOTION

Redemption is birth
You have spent days in burning hell
Wanting back on earth
    –Daquan Horton

Don't use H$_2$O
There is no dryer for it
Drugs will never help
    –Daquan Horton

He stands on the roof
Everyone's there, mouths moving
"Stop Now" a girl says
    –Charity Chakwa

I don't like people
Hugs and party times are great
Feelings intertwine
    –Charity Chakwa

The river is very sight
The river is a sign of peace
The world can have peace
    –Breona Meniefield

The grass is so green
Nature needs to be very very clean
Nature is good in spring
    –Breona Meniefield

THE BIRTH OF SUCCESS

The peace is broken
When people kill others just because
The peace is broken
   —Jasmine Jones

Peace is a river
The river is flowing fast
We're swimming through it
   —I'Nyah Wright

My color is so green
Green is the color of the grass
That's why I love green
   —I'Nyah Wright

I am so hungry
I don't want to starve to death
I am so hungry
   —Rashad Young

I like to eat food
Chicken is my favorite food
That's why I love food
   —Rashad Young

POETRY IN MOTION

I love to have money
No day goes by without money
I am married to money
    –Tony Hopkins

Dead society
Our secrets have been figured out
What have we become!
    –Iyana Thompson

The gun is ready
Going steady his heart beats
Decided to live
    –Iyana Thompson

When you smoke you die
When you drink and drive you die
Go ahead and try; BYE
    –Ariana Gatlin

Snickers are the best
The caramel and chocolate it is complete
Snickers are the best
    –Ariana Gatlin

54 THE BIRTH OF SUCCESS

THE BIRTH OF SUCCESS

WDC Youth Poetry Slam Team Members perform for DTWT: Eric Powell, Oyunde, Mr. Malcom

Local Rap Artist Slim Tristan spends day with DTWT Youth discussing music industry

Final Picture with Slim Tristan

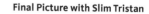

Poetry Slam Team member Malcom performs

ANTI BULLYING POEMS

DO THE WRITE THING SYEP ANTI-BULLYING CAMPAIGN

Bullying

It's happening all around
Throwing kids on the ground
Physical, emotional, cyber and verbal
It's a huge problem,
not just a little hurdle
Kids should not have to have this fear
They shouldn't have to cry a tear
They should sleep peacefully through the night
And not have to put up a fight
Crying tears and bloodshed
We need to stand up and get
this message spread
Kids shouldn't feel this low
And have marks to show.
Stop Bullying

STOP Bullying now

The Problem: Bullying occurs among school children as young as six years old. Twelve per cent of 10-year-olds report they were bullied "about weekly" (*International Association for Evaluation of Educational Achievement, 2012*). During adolescence about 30% of pupils are bullied in any half-term period (*Anti-Bullying Center, 2013*).

Fifty–five per cent of young people report being bullied (UNICEF Report: *Changing the Future, 2012*). Bullying has a well-documented and very serious negative impact in both the short term and the long term on targeted pupils. Left unchecked, it can also lead to negative outcomes for unreformed bullies with 60% of boys involved having a criminal conviction by age 24 and 35% of boys involved having at least three such convictions (Dan Olweus, 1993).

In the long run, then, bullying is bad for everyone involved and everyone stands to benefit if it can be prevented or reduced. I conducted workshops on bullying and asked youth to write poems on the topic in order to provide an outlet for those who may have encountered such abuse, or who wished to express their concerns about it. Please join DTWT in this campaign against bullying in the District of Columbia and anywhere else in the world.

Marion Duane Ingram

M. Duane Ingram
Executive Director
Do The Write Thing of DC

ANTI-BULLYING POEM

Timothy Bey

Bullying hurts, don't you see?
You are nothing, but a big bully
Don't you think of what could have been?
What if they put a razor to their skin?

What if they wrote a note to say goodbye?
And their family and friends were left wondering...why?
What if at night, they cry themselves to sleep?
By morning, it's too hard to get up on their feet

They are afraid to come to school because of bullies like you
When they try to tell an adult, their plead is overruled
Soon they can't take it anymore
They think, "What do I have to live for?"

Finally all of their secrets start to spill
They grab the bottle and overdose on pills
All they ever wanted was a friend
And to hear the words, "I'm sorry, I won't do it again"

You did it all for the fun
You didn't know what could've been done
What if you pushed them a bit too far?
All your actions have caused one big scar

Haven't you seen what you put them through?
You think they're weak, but they're stronger than you
All they want to do is forget
They think, "how much worse can it get?"

Don't you know, you're their biggest fear?
They scream so loud, but no one can hear
What if it was you who got hurt every day?
Tell me how many words you would have left to say

ANTI-BULLYING POEM

Aziza Withers

Bullying is never okay
It is often always mean in a harmful way
Some people may take it a different way
It's still in harm's way.
Some people may get suicidal
Some people may get genocidal
Some people bully people their own idol.

ANTI-BULLYING POEM II

Aziza Withers

I walk into the school building they stare,
they point,
they laugh,
I cry inside.

As I walk down the hall a girl trips me,
I fall, everything in my bag come out.
my laptop falls out on top,
the girl takes a water bottle,
opens it and tips it over,
I have no more laptop.

I walk on,
they spit in my direction,
I walk into class,
I go to sit down in my assigned seat,
gum is stuck onto the seat,
I take a napkin and try to get it all off,

the bell rings,
class starts,
the passing of the notes begins,
each one gets nastier and meaner.

BULLYING POEM

Keonte Townsend

So he just tortures himself as he has no fortune and wealth
He extorts someone else to get his dough
Now he's acting like a bully
He tries to push and pull me
He know that he can't fool me
He's mad he has no choice but to scream
He raises his voice up at me cause it annoys him to see that I am not scared

ANTI-BULLYING POEM

George Anderson

Bullying is not right
Often cause people to fight.

Emotions are hidden
Being embarrassed should be forbidden

Bullies prey on the weak
Don't be weak be strong

Seem alone but all along
You're just afraid to sing the song

Afraid to say what's wrong
In the meanwhile others are singing the song.

ANTI-BULLYING POEM

Damoni Tolson

You never know how bullying feels until it happens to you
It never happened to me
I wouldn't allow it
I have seen it many times
I don't step in unless it's a friend
But, then again if it was me I would want help from anyone
But, then again I wouldn't allow it
So I wouldn't understand the pain that victims feel

ANTI-BULLYING POEM

Mic'Quon Contee

Live It Right
If you're a bully you might as well
kill yourself because it seems you really don't care

If you're a bully you mustn't care about anyone's health
The world should care more about bullying then personal wealth

When you're at your father's house yes he's hitting you with a belt
Maybe that's why you bully others from pain of self

So bully I dare you to come try me
You might become missing
Or be in a hospital
Hooked up to an IV

ANTI-BULLYING POEM

Joseph Hailey

Tortured soul passed by
He looked sad I asked why?

He said my imperfection
can't be correction so I

Don't know why
they tease me so and then

He cried the tortured soul
was dead the next week

It was a suicide case
killed by a blade in his own hand in his place

ANTI-BULLYING POEM

Keonte Townsend

I never got bullied before. I hope not to.
I've seen somebody get bullied the other day.
Sometimes people got to fight back.
You would never know what I have been through.
Bullying is a sign of hating and getting new

ANTI-BULLYING POEM

Charnisha Brown

Why would you want to be a bully,
When you know you're an angel truly,
Physical and emotional bullying
Your actions don't only mislead you,
They have others feeling ashamed too,
I would rather be a little nobody,
than to be so evil it both hurts
It's dangerous and affects a lot of lives
It's like your face and feelings being stuffed in dirt.
Bullying is like breaking out in hives.

ANTI-BULLYING POEM

Sydney McKenzie

Bullies. Smh. Yeah I know what those are.
tear drops, eyes closed, a faint feeling in my heart.

I can't say I don't see what it feels like
I see the sorrow and desperation in their eyes.

Why are you so angry when theres no reason to be?
A hurt person in a bad situation is what he or she seems

Yeah I know exactly what you are
You feel empty, as small as a star

Mhm yeah you're small & lack power, something you need
satisfaction of hurting a person, yeah you're a bully.

MAKE IT THROUGH

Tymia Bailey

I know this is not my fate
God put me here for a reason

So now it's my duty to please
By going through all the pain

People putting me to shame
Making me wish I die

So I can be with my loved ones in the sky
But I will not break

For my loved one's sake
I will feel pain but won't show it

So I'll go through it until God says it's time for a change
And end all my pain

ANTI-BULLYING POEM

Toni Hawkins

Bullying needs to stop
It causes people to pop

It causes so much pain
And drives people insane

It makes life terrible
To the point that it's unbearable

It makes you resort to cutting
And you end up shutting down

The bullying need to cease
Or the death rate will increase

ANTI-BULLYING POEM

Amony Johnson

From the first time she rolled her eyes
at me and said something slick under her breath
I knew that this was a test
to see if I would do anything
but I didn't 'cause I was kinda a goodie goodie
So I wouldn't ever fight a bully
Then there was lunch and she sat in front of me
It was kinda hard to believe
until I got up for a sec and came back
and saw someone took my fruit snacks

ANTI-BULLYING POEM

Paprika Berry

Motionless I stand as a million people
pass me, I'm in a place full of life but I'm dead.

Not literally but emotionally,
Everyone's moving so fast,
They don't even realize that I'm not moving.

I look down at my watch;
And just like me the minute hand is still.

I rather them pass me than to notice me
When they do see me, it's always bad
Because every day they wish I was dead.

ANTI-BULLYING POEM

Christopher Tate

Bullying causes a
double threat in life
both physical and
emotional bullying are wrong
Bullies bully because they
are full of anger and depression
Confession about bullying
can help redeem themselves as a better person
but the people we need to worry are
the people who need freedom from being bullied

ANTI-BULLYING POEM

Maurice Edwards

Pain/Words
Hurts me when I think about
Makes me wanna cry

The last time they messed with me
I wished they died

Eyes red you could see the steam off my head
I was so mad I couldn't go home to my bed

Walked the streets to clear my head
Thinking back to the pain and torture I was fed

Words haunt me and ring in my ear
Wish I could share with my peers

You talk about me and think you're cool
But really joke's on you you're the fool

Revenge will only make it worse
But one day you will feel my pain & hurt

ANTI-BULLYING POEM

Terin Collins

Bullying is like a rite of passage
But there is only so much bullying you can manage

Through pain and turmoil a lesson is to be learned
It's that true freedom that is to be earned

Bullying is a deadly game to be played
Through hateful emotions decisions swayed

Taunting and harassing, messing with emotions
Confusion and question, why is this my poison

But still I rise, above to the top
With God on my side, striving I'll never stop.

ANTI-BULLYING POEM

Nya Morton

I guess bullying is a way for people to let off steam
Or they may just suffer from low self esteem
People think that bullying makes them look like thugs and G's
A bully can torture someone or hurt them with ease

A bully's word can hurt like a punch to the chest
They love to knock someone down when they
      see them at their best.
Hurtful words and forceful blows to the dome
Learning kids crying and hanging themselves in their homes.

They say only sticks and stones can break your bones
But the words of a bully hurt just as much as those
Bullying hurts feelings and also hurts pride
They either leave you with bruises or eternal pain on the inside.

ANTI-BULLYING POEM

Kyndall Jones

Him

You see him and you know something's wrong.
But he's your best friend and he would tell you anything.
You never questioned why he always flinched when you
    hugged him.
Or why he never ate around you.
Your head didn't turn when he wore long sleeves in the summer.
You always believed him when he said he was okay.
Yesterday he told you he loved you. You said it back and shrugged
it off because you thought he was acting weird.
He didn't come back the next day.
Or the next.
So you went to his house.
In his room he was there.
Hanging from the ceiling fan.
You finally saw that he wasn't okay.
That the rainbow of bruises actually meant something was up.
The slashes on his arm were his reason for long sleeves.
The flinching from his abuse.
His pain.

Now he's gone.

And it's too late to help.

ANTI-BULLYING POEM

Keva Iracks

You should know, bullying hurts.
It starts with one word, one word you blurt.
Fat, ugly, worthless. These are the words they hear.
Did you know, you're their biggest fear?

ANTI-BULLYING POEM

Andre Amalemba

Picking fights is something that can't be prevented.
But bullying is the thing that excels it.

People are dying due to the threat
What started harmless all but ended with a bet

The silent ones are the deadly ones
The ones that nobody can call

Those long forgotten never to be gotten
Only to be lost to nothing but a fault

ANTI-BULLYING POEM

Daschmiere Fenwick

It took me only a few years for me to realize
I couldn't shed anymore tears.
So I took a blade but didn't cut so deep.
I could never imagine it getting that far
in only a few years.
Thought about throwing them away
but it was something I wanted to keep.
Memories of feeling worthless
Started to think my life was purposeless
What did I ever go wrong
I never understood so I would just go home
cry and listen to my favorite song.
I thought they liked me
But it didn't stop them from making fun
of the gap between my teeth.
I just fought my way through things
Didn't really know how to act
but how I look back
And say "wow" I never thought I'd make
it through that.

ANTI-BULLYING POEM

Aisha Ferguson

Lost words
Loose ties

The things I said
destroyed my mind

Scaring glares
anger flares

Thinking just
doesn't happen here

This drama of being bullied

ANTI-BULLYING POEM

Destiny Sanders

It's not good to bully
It's not good to be a bully it's silly just worry about
how you see yourself in the future with a cup milly
It's not fully the right thing
Not nice, it isn't right
NO BULLY ZONE
should be the new tone
It's not good to be a bully fully it's just silly
It's stupid
Forever looped
To repeat itself forever
Pain, fear, tears
Again & again

TALE OF A TORTURED SOUL

MyKalyah Ware

Fist clenched
eyes closed

Breathing heavy
stuffed nose

A dark room
a lonely corner

Dangerous mind
all alone

Arm cut, bleeding out
blade bloody, rusting about

Pain illuminating
suffering radiating

Silent cries
depression fought

Your bullying affected me
more than you thought

ANTI-BULLYING POEM

Jalon Rowe

You should know, bullying hurts.
It starts with one word, one word you blurt.
Fat, ugly, worthless. These are the words they hear.
Did you know, you're their biggest fear?

Day by day you torment them,
it takes so long for their hearts to mend.
All they ask for is one true friend,
but you make them want their lives to end.

Everyday they wake up with regret,
all they want to do is forget.
It's not just hitting and punching, it's the words you say,
they hurt so much, they want to fade away.

This is when enough is enough,
they're sick of playing strong, sick of playing tough.
But they know they can make it through,
you may not have known, but they always knew.

They put on a fake smile and pretend they're okay,
they believe they can make it all the way.
Of course your words still offend,
but they have been pieced back together again.

Someone leaves the crowd and lends them a hand,
they learn that it's time to stand.
Their smile is no longer fake,
now they have no reason to ache.

You see, all they ever needed was a friend,
someone to stand by them when the bullying came again.
Now they are free,
the insults barely sting, don't you see?

ANTI-BULLYING POEM

Tanika Garner

Bullying is bad. It will make you sad
You need to stop and make someone glad

Bullying is so upsetting it will make you cry
If you're a bully please don't lie if you make someone die

Bullying will hurt your feelings so people need to get on the top
Bullying causes you to get injured and it's not good
       so it needs to stop

Bullying is negative behavior that causes other people strife
If you're a bully you need to stop before someone ends
       their own life

It's just stupid so try to do good like make love arrows like cupid.

ANTI-BULLYING POEMS

Ciera Oliver

As I make my way to school each day
To see the girls who break my soul
I wish I could tell the bullies in my school
Can you be kind and not so cruel?

And it starts and lasts all day
I cannot stand it, go away
Just close your eyes and you will see
All the memories that you have engraved in me

I think to myself
There is no pain, there is no fear
So dry away that silent tear
It's not that easy you must know

I'm not a project of anybody
I'm not your pity either for you to be my friend
Give me a chance so you can see
There is nothing strange about me

That you have not let them see
I ask myself will this ever end?
I just feel empty time to time inside me
Sooner or later I'll break down and cry

Let the darkness fill the room
I can't get out of it, I can't resume
I feel so alone like a single red rose,
So alone like a story that's never been told
I feel so alone like a sparrow in the sky
Like a bird who cannot fly

I am lucky to have a family like mine
Who understand me and feel pride
Otherwise my world would be dark
With every unpleasant memories
That is left inside me.

Never allow anyone to bring you down
On your mind make these feelings
Make you stronger and put your head up high
Never keep it silent
There is nothing to feel ashamed of
Only to those that join in all that harm.

As I get up in the morning
To prepare myself for school
My body and my mind
Start to get scared and
My life felt very dark inside
I couldn't take it any longer

As I started to share my pain with my mum
I didn't know how to explain to her
It all came out with tears and a broken heart

She couldn't comprehend as I hid it for a while
I showed her every day I was a happy child
Nobody will understand that bullying can make such harm
I ask myself everyday what wrong have I done

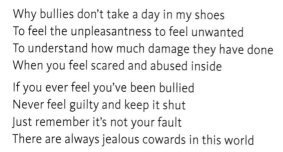

Why bullies don't take a day in my shoes
To feel the unpleasantness to feel unwanted
To understand how much damage they have done
When you feel scared and abused inside

If you ever feel you've been bullied
Never feel guilty and keep it shut
Just remember it's not your fault
There are always jealous cowards in this world

ANTI-BULLYING POEM

Craig Washington

Think of life as one big plate
one side they love, one side they hate

For all the rubbish you give us, all day and all night
we never get the chance to defend or fight

So now it's our chance to stand up and say "NO!"
maybe you'll have to leave without us having to go!

80 THE BIRTH OF SUCCESS

WHERE I'M FROM

THE BIRTH OF SUCCESS

WHERE I'M FROM

Dajeh Johnson

Where I'm from I hear gunshots
Where I'm from we eat takis
Where I'm from we do drugs
Where I'm from we carry straps
Where I'm from we pop gum
Where I'm from there's ratchetness

WHERE I'M FROM

Charnisha Brown

Where I'm from, you hear noise louder than a drum
Where I'm from, parents act careless and dumb
Where I'm from, most fathers are bums
Where I'm from, it's never the time to come

Where I'm from, chewing gum without sharing isn't yum
Where I'm from, people will sit on the porch while sippin' Rum
Where I'm from, people will beg for chump change with
      an anger rage.
Where I'm from, age is just a number. It leaves a lot of wonder
Where I'm from, nobody is safe even with a grape

I'm from Washington D.C.
something similar to a dead sea

WHERE I'M FROM

Tymia Bailey

Where I'm from, people send shots to one another
Where I'm from, kids' life are taking from their mother
Where I'm from, kids sell weed on the streets
Where I'm from there's always hood beef
Where I'm from you're never safe
Where I'm from your friend will have people run up
    in your own place
Where I'm from is a place I don't like to claim because
so many people like to cause others pain
Where I'm from is a place I would like to stay away from.

WHERE I'M FROM

Author Unknown

Where I'm from you'll get popped in the head
Where I'm from we don't play no games
Where I'm from you gotta watch your back no matter what
Where I'm from nobody gives a flying flick
Where I'm from dealers always in the gutter
Where I'm from crack heads ask for money
Where I'm from we shoot, hit, and run
I'm from Brooklyn where no games are played and
    cops get slayed

WHERE I'M FROM

Asia Thorne

Welcome to Brooklyn
the great big hood of New York
Where dreams and stars fly

Oh yeah she jealous
trynna link up by the park
I been there done that

Your heart beats faster
you know he/she the one
When you love someone

WHERE I'M FROM

D'Angelo Holley

Where I'm from everybody gamble
Where I'm from everybody say they real
Where I'm from everybody think they from Chiraq
Where I'm from everybody gotta eat
Where I'm from everybody smoke pack
Where I'm from everybody scream omerta
Where I'm from it's called the capitol
Capitol of our nation
We are important
We are overlooked
We are a family
in many ways

Where I'm from we are strong
Where I'm from produces leaders
Where I'm from is the land of the great

WHERE I'M FROM

Jalon Rowe

Where I'm from you can go out and play ball
Where I'm from we break ankles and people fall
Where I'm from houses are spread apart and good amount of land
Where I'm from you can walk and sit all day like you on the beach
 in cozy sand
Where I'm from there is no tragic
Where I'm from little kids outside watching magicians do magic
Where I'm from it's like living in Bloomingdale
Where I'm from you're riding name brand bikes Cannondale
Where I'm from it's good to be
Where I'm from you will never want to leave.

WHERE I'M FROM

Aujanae Barnum

You hear children playing
you see people walking calmly
you see a whole lot of green
you see many buildings like Raw house
You see mothers & children walking side by side
You see a whole lot but that's where I'm from.

Clerihew

88 THE BIRTH OF SUCCESS

CLERIHEW POEMS

Charnisha Brown

Beyoncé
Brave, flawless
Talented, dashing diva
Perfect regardless
Beautiful

R. Kelly
Breath is smelly
like pork belly
no better than Nelly
or petroleum jelly

Lil Wayne
Raps insane
still remains
best rapper in the fast lane

Miley Cyrus
Is like a virus
sometimes stylish
but a total minus

Lil MaMa
Raps like she from the Bahamas with drama
without a comma
looking like Obama

CLERIHEW POEMS

Nya Morton

Jay-Z
Had nowhere to flee
When Beyoncé's sis
Tried to kick him in the penis

Nicki Minaj, female MC
Also known as "harijuku Barbie"
Knows that she's the best
Because of her rhymes and her assets

CLERIHEW POEMS

Rajae Jackson

Nicki Minaj is whack
she got a fat back
her face look like snot
but her butt is phat

Chris Brown look good
he don't claim no hood
he from VA
he be with trey

CLERIHEW POEMS

Dajeh Johnson

Jay-Z

married to Beyoncé and became lazy
his game is crazy
and he is a little hazy

Beyoncé

was once popular
but then she married Jay-Z
and now she's binocular

CLERIHEW POEMS

Asia Thorne

Lil Wayne

he looks like he needs a cane
he ain't got no money to gain

Chris Rock

Boy please
wanted to be on the BET awards so bad
he got on his knees
I think Kevin Hart should have the cup

CLERIHEW POEMS

Modane Robinson

Lil Wayne

got all the game
he stay going to jail
but he got money for the bail.

CLERIHEW POEMS

Jailyn Sekou

Erykah Badu

only speaks what's true
sometimes she makes music that
can relate to you and your boo
fixes days that may be blue

Wale

gives you songs you can listen
to everyday
he spits rhymes that helps you
go in the right way
he makes those gray days
go away

Peace love war money faith
all things essential to life we make
what it means to you?

Love nothing is above this
the feelings, the person, and the bliss
blissful thoughts that fill your mind

CLERIHEW POEMS

MyKaylah Ware

Brendo Vrie

sounds of fury
the songs he sing
with the lines Dallon brings

Pete Wentz

sounds of heaven
the things he sings
a pure eleven

CLERIHEW POEMS

Tymia Bailey

Have you heard of Drake
throwing bottles at light skins how fake
Luckily, you got a good aim
Because if he would've got to you
    he would have ended your fame

Barack Obama
encouraged my mama
to stay strong
but he won't be in the White House for long

CLERIHEW POEMS

Toni Hawkins

Lil Wayne
He's such a pain
He thinks he's insane
When really he's lame

Megan Fox
Lives in a box
She doesn't where socks
And should grow dreadlocks

I watch TV a lot
Adventure time very cool
Watch it all the time

Enjoying drawing
I like to draw graffiti
It entertains me

Visual Haiku

THE BIRTH OF SUCCESS

HAIKU POEMS

Charnisha Brown

Peace Haiku

An eye for an eye
doesn't comply anything
It makes the word blind.

Love Haiku

Love is in the air
who can really compare
with a great meaning.

HAIKU POEM

Author Unknown

The freedom fighters
Peacemakers have peace of mind
everyday mending

Washington D.C.
very dangerous species
outstanding city

HAIKU POEMS

Tymia Bailey

You're behind them bars
because you caused people pain
now things aren't the same

Calm everyone down
end all the pain with a hug
we should share the love

D.C. is so loud
because people are so proud
But we are different

HAIKU POEM

Asia Thorne

See the trees and bees
the flowers bloom with great ease
The fish flow in peace

HAIKU POEM

Paprika Berry

Sun beaming on down,
Where the days don't end till late,
No time better than this.

You're not alone,
Even when they are mean to you,
Know that we are here.

HAIKU POEMS

Daschmiere Fenwick

I don't watch football.
It is so stupid to me.
I don't watch football.

I am not happy.
I act like it sometimes though.
I wish I could be.

HAIKU POEM

Troy Williams

spring wakens my tree
a bejeweled perfumed bride.
love birds make their nest
in my tree's sombrero

summer's yellowed lawn beneath
a grass breathes sweetly in air
in a cracked bathroom

MY MORNING EPIPHANY

Afia Tyus

Woke up one morning
I saw the impossible
And I looked past it

TO THE BULLY

I say close your eyes
And put yourself in their place
Then see how it feels

Free Verse & Short Stories

102 **THE BIRTH OF SUCCESS**

MAYBE

Makaylah Ware

Maybe I should smile
It doesn't have to be real
I could just fake it

I want the wind to go
talking the cherry blossom
to the world unknown

I will drop my blade
satisfaction from the pain
I no longer need

Love really does hurt
It pains me to think of it
I don't need any

When I want to be
A place where I am happy
Not here in D.C.

My stomach clenched
and my heart pace

My fists were balled
but my thoughts were flat

No one was going to help

I wanted to cry
but that would make me weak

Right?

I wanted to disappear
to go away

but where do you go when you have nowhere to go

It was endless
the situation
But when it ended
It was broken bliss
But I was still damaged

SILENT SUICIDE

Makaylah Ware

I think you missed the signs.
The late nights,
Weary eyes,
Meals skipped,
Walking forced.
Yeah. You missed them.
The anti-socialness of
avoiding large crowds
low voice
the missing eye contact
The suspicious cuts down the arm
From the imaginary cat
Yet, when you see the screen,
when you hear the tragedy,
of a suicide teen
You think:
"What happened?
They were so happy"
No. You're wrong.
You missed the signs
Which made this
A silent suicide
Don't you know, you're their biggest fear?

They scream so loud, but no one can hear
What if it was you who got hurt everyday?
Tell me how many words you would have left to say

ME

Makaylah Ware

I do what I can,
What I can must,
Held by that standard,
Yet betrayed by trust,
In a crowd
yet a single soft whisper you heard.

Hold my hand,
cry the pain
Then take reign
Of the kingdom that's rightfully yours.
Stand up tall
And claim
from once you came

Easier said than done
Or so they say
Elaborated as fun
as entertain
Yet all the humor is taken away

Take my hand;
Let's run forward
Where gray wasn't augured
Colors are gone
And black and white rule
Bring forth the truth
Held back by truth

SOMETHING FROM NOTHING:

Makaylah Ware

Okay I might not be the strongest.
Or the fastest.
Or the smartest.
Or the coolest.
But you know what I do have?
Nothing.
Not a thing.
Like absolute zero

They say you can't multiply nothing
That you'll only get nothing.
They're right.
Anything times nothing is nothing
So I'm not going to make myself 10 times better
Or 20 times better
Instead I'm going to add on to what I already have.
Add on to nothing.
If you add on to nothing you get something.

Right?
That's what I'm going to do.
I'm going to add on.
A little there.
A bit here.
A tiny piece anywhere.
And it's going to take me a while.
I mean come on, I started at nothing.

But my nothing will get there.
Get to the heights that my nothing never dreamed possible.
My nothing will go from not a thing to it all.
Not because I multiply it, no I added on

But I won't add too much.
Because I might just fall.
Back to nothing.

SHORT STORY FOR SEMI-REGULAR TALE OF A GIRL & A BOY

Makaylah Ware

"This is all the Wolf's fault!" Anna muttered. He had to get a job at the castle. He had to be successful. He had to get promoted to the king's personal guard. He just had to get invited to a stupid ball and she just had to go. She was tugging on the neckline of the gown she was wearing; it was suffocating. The seamstress glared at her and slapped her hand away.

"Let me finish!" She exclaimed. Anna bit her bottom lip and the seamstress got back to work.

"So who do you plan to dance with?" The lady asked as her fingers worked skillfully at the hems of the gown. Anna snorted at the question.

"No one. I plan to be in the shadows; where no one can see me," she said. The seamstress shook her head. She looked up at Anna and gave her a smile.

"You're going to look beautiful." She said, "You'll have all the fellows wanting to dance with you in this dress." She hummed as she went along.

"But what if I don't want to dance with people?" Anna asked. She didn't like the thought of dancing with random people.

"The blue of the gown goes nicely with your dark hair and grey eyes," the lady said. She said with such excitement in her voice that Anna could tell she loved her job....

After thirty more minutes the gown was complete. And not a moment too soon; the ball was in an hour. A maid came in to usher Anna out and into another room where a different woman would do her hair and makeup.

When will this torture end?! Anna thought.

The maid sat Anna down on a stool.

"Lady Ameira will be here shortly to dress your hair and makeup," she said. She gave a short curtsy before leaving the room. A minute later the door opened again and a middle aged woman came in.

"Are you Annaliese?" The woman asked. Anna inwardly groaned.

Anna! She wanted to shout at the lady, my name is Anna!

Wolf told her when in doubt do what you usually wouldn't do. So Anna gave the woman a polite smile and nodded.

"Yes Ma'am," she said in her most polite voice, "I'm Anna. Are you Lady Ameira?" The woman regarded Anna for a second and nodded.

"Turn around in the seat," Ameira said, picking up the comb. Anna's hair was still a little damp from the bath she took in the morning. If Lady Ameira noticed she didn't comment on it.

She ran the comb through Anna's hair getting out all of the kinks and tangles and knots. Anna knew that it would be awhile before Ameira finished so she let her mind wander.

It wasn't always like this. Living in a big castle, attending balls, being waited on night and day. It use to be her and Wolf and their parents living in a small cabin in the woods. They had no money and their father worked a lot in the city, selling wood. Then one day misfortune struck. Their mother died in childbirth, the baby as well. It was a devastating blow. Their father was too sad to work so Wolf had to chop the wood and sell it. Over time things didn't get better. Their father's health diminished and death soon took him, too. Wolf continued to work while Anna stayed home alone.

Then fortune smiled. Wolf saved the life of the crown prince. As a reward the king gave him a job as one of his personal guards. Then they moved to this big castle.

Anna hated it. She missed when the family was alive and happy together.

Anna was so lost in the past that she barely noticed Ameira calling her name.

"Annaliese!" Ameira exclaimed. Anna blinked once and looked up at the woman.

"Yes?" She asked. Ameira tapped her foot impatiently. In her hands she held a mirror.

"Do you not respond to your own name?" She snapped. She held the mirror out for Anna to see the end result.

Anna had to admit; she looked beautiful. Her face was still pale as ever but Ameira had reddened her cheeks. Her eyes were shadowed blue and her lips a soft pink. Her hair laid in ringlets around her head. Anna looked up at Ameira. She opened her mouth once but nothing came out. She had no idea what to say.

"A simple 'thank you' would suffice," Ameira said peevishly, as if she could read Anna's mind. There was a knock at the door before Anna could reply. Ameira sighed.

"Come in!" She called. The door opened and Wolf stepped in. He was dressed in his guard uniform. Ameira put on a charming smile and sauntered over to him.

"Why hello, Sir Avert," she purred. Wolf nodded towards her. He paid her little attention. Instead he was grinning at his little sister.

"Why Ann!" He exclaimed, "You look like a girl!" Anna felt her face burn up and she glared up.

"Be quiet!" She said, standing up. Ameira shot Anna a look of disapproval but Anna ignored it.

Wolf held out his arm.

"Shall we?" He said with mocking politeness. Anna gave him a grin and took his arm.

"Lead the way." They left out the room, leaving Ameira without another word.

Anna couldn't be more nervous. She and Wolf waited on the top of the stairs, waiting for the servant to announce their name. Wolf looked down at her.

"Anna," he said in a low voice so that only she could hear. There were lots of different people around, ranking from dukes to barons. Anyone who was anyone was there.

"Don't worry," he said, "I won't leave your side." Then the servant called them.

"Wolfram and Annaliese of the Avert family," he called down the stairs. Wolf nudged Anna forward. Anna took a deep breath and walked.

The room hushed as Anna and Wolf walked down. When they reached the bottom they crowded around Wolf, pushing Anna away from him. He reached helpless after her.

So much for sticking by my side, she thought. But she knew it wasn't his fault. He was popular and unmarried. Of course he'd have a swarm of girls around him. She decided to take this time to be alone.

"Hey! Anna!" Someone called. She knew that high pitched voice. A voice that belonged to a person she so dreaded. She plastered a fake smile on her face and turned around.

"Mary!" She exclaimed. She opened her arms and they briefly hugged. Mary looked back to the big crowd-of girls-surrounding Wolf.

"So," Mary said, whispering, "What's the status on Wolfram? Is he... engaged?" Anna looked at Wolf and back at Mary. He didn't need a girl like her. She was mean, selfish, and cared only for her own well-being.

"Yes," she whispered, "he is. But it's a secret!" She knew that Mary wouldn't keep a secret. Good. She could go tell her friends and so forth and they would finally leave Wolf alone. Before Mary could return Anna left. She headed towards a secluded corner.

"Anna!"

She mentally groaned. This voice was deeper, and male.

It was Adam, son of some count whose name she couldn't care to remember. She threw up another fake smile.

"Adam! Hi!" She said as though she was happy to see him. He gave her what he thought was a charming smile.

"Hello Anna, how are you?" He asked. Anna looked over to where Wolf was. It wasn't in the same direction as the corner she was headed to but she needed an excuse.

"I'm sorry, Adam," she said, "I think Wolf is calling for me!" Adam searched the room for Wolf. He spotted him. When he turned back to Anna she had already walked away, in a different direction.

"Anna!" He called. He pointed to Wolf, "Your brother is that way!" Anna didn't turn around.

"I know that," she muttered to herself. "Just wanted to get away from you." There was nothing wrong with Adam. She just didn't like him the way he seemed to like her. Though she was pretty sure that he just wanted a loveless marriage. There was no point in marriage if it didn't have love. But she was still fourteen and young; she'd worry about that in upcoming years.

Soon she reached the corner. It was dimly lit and no one was around. She leaned against the wall and slid down. Finally she was alone...

"What are you doing here alone?" Someone asked. She sighed. Whoever this was she wanted gone. But she didn't recognize this voice so she looked up. A tall boy looked down at her.

"Who are you?" She asked. He raised an eyebrow.

"I asked you a question first," he said. Anna rolled her eyes. As if she cared he asked her a question first.

"Answer me and I'll answer you," she said, going for a compromise. The boy smirked and pointed at the little crown of gold resting on top of his mane of brown hair. Anna opened her mouth then closed it.

"I... I'm," she tried to but she couldn't find the right words.

The prince chuckled.

"Don't laugh at me!" She snapped, "You could've just answered my question when I asked." He nodded.

"Aye, I could have but most people know who I am," he pointed out. Anna blushed and crossed her arms. She had heard of the crown prince, just never saw or met him until now…

"I'm not most people."

He grinned.

"I can tell."

He sat down next to her and stuck out his hand.

"Cathel," he said, introducing himself. She looked at him then his hand. She grabbed it.

"Anna."

They shook hands.

SILENT ATTACKER

By Kyndall Jones

It is a cold dark night. A man silently creeps into a home of a middle aged woman. He'd been watching her for a week now, he knew she lived alone. He waits until she lies in her bed to attack her. He stabs the woman in her hip and watches her gargle on her own blood, a precious new victim. The woman flails uselessly in fear, perhaps as a last resort. He smiles to himself seeing how ridiculous this woman was acting. The woman tries to crawl towards the bedroom door but he grabs her and drags her back to the kitchen. She screams loudly as if anyone could save her now. He stabs her a final time in her back. Within minutes the woman ceases breathing and lies, glass eyed, and face down on the blood stained floor. He flips the woman over and begins cutting open her chest. He cuts open her stomach to examine what she had for dinner, spaghetti

and meatballs. He cuts out her eye to keep for sentimental value. He did this with all of his victims just as a memory of his successful kills. The woman's eye was a sheer cornflower blue. He loved that color, he thought it looked beautiful. It reminded him of the peaceful days before he started killing. But still not as beautiful as blood. He loved the metallic smell, the deep red color, and the thick texture. He dipped his finger in her blood and tasted itches smiled rolling his tongue on its flavor, he determined that she had AB+ blood. Her blood was sweet and dry. Just the way he liked it. Killing people was his entire world. Nothing else ever mattered to him. Hearing screams of terror was invigorating. Watching the life slowly drain from his victims was orgasmic. He loved every single aspect there was to killing. For his trademark, he took out a flower. A ghost orchid. Also one of the rarest flowers in the world. He set it directly in her mouth, making it look as if it were growing there. Then he left just as silently as he'd come.

IF YOU COULD CHANGE ANYTHING

Afia Tyus

I've been asked,
If you could change anything in your life right now what would you change?
Now that's a loaded question,
With answers beyond my capacity.
But first thing that comes to my mind
Is sleep.
Sleep.
5 letters
1 sound
1 action

Simple, right?
Go to bed early,
Sleep the whole weekend
But life goes on even if you're asleep
A simple fact
That changes my whole philosophy of sleep.
And then I start to think of everything that can go wrong with sleep
That simple 5 letter word with 1 sound
Grades, Attitude, Anxiety, Social behavior, Depression.
Your happiness.

Such a valuable thing to lose.
When you're deciding
To sleep or be social,
To rest or to learn,
Ugh!
And I write ugh without the right word to
describe my state of mind right now
The scream that rages within me every day over something
I thought was simple.
Sleep.

So in the event that I can't sleep,
Here's what happens
I close my mouth,
And I watch everything unfold before my eyes.
And think to myself maybe today is that day I'll figure it out,
The key to my own happiness.
But for now
I cry
To find a way to settle that emotion that won't go away
That won't be quiet during every second of every minute

And if I could close my heart I wouldn't feel it all.
But I do feel and I do cry.
Not because of everything going on in my life,
Or the rest of the world around me.
But, because I can't sleep.

STEREOTYPE

Toni Hawkins

Everybody...is...stereotyped. Not realizing that we're all just people. Just because my skin is black and yours is white doesn't make us any different. You say I'm inferior because of my skin color and because of yours you have more intelligence. Well that's not the case, that's not how I see it. I see us ALL as equals yet you see me as a thug, a criminal when that's not true at all. But what is true is that I can overcome the beliefs you have about me due to my skin color. Just because he's a little lighter and she's a little darker doesn't make us any different so why are we treated as such. Stereotypes they shape and form how we view one another yet the only difference is I'm treated like nothing. When not treated as a stereotype your treated like a king, or a God when really were all just people. People that are trying to make it by in life. People who are trying to succeed, so why? Why is it that I'm treated like dirt? Why does everyone believe in you and not me? One word, eleven letters: STEREOTYPE.

NO MORE!!!

Toni Hawkins

Your words shall hurt me no longer
Because all the pain you caused made me stronger
I used to crawl into a corner crying my eyes away
Wondering what went wrong that certain day
But now I see the true light in you
You have pain also, but you thought no one knew
You don't have to cause others pain
Just to hide all your shame.....

ACTIONS

Toni Hawkins

You didn't think your words would hurt
But now look a little girl is buried in the dirt
You didn't even notice the cuts that lie upon her arm
Because all the pain you caused
Now her family is grieving because of their loss
She decided that there was a need for change
So she took her life away so she couldn't feel no more pain
I hope you decide that bullying is not a good choice to make
Because it just might put peoples' lives at stake

UNIQUE

Toni Hawkins

What makes what I'm doing
Any different from the person next to me?
Or the person next to her,
Or the people in this school.
What makes me unique?

Because, I see clones.
Do I have on the 3-D glasses?
Am I the one who's wrong?
It might just be me.
And I'm cool with that
But take a second and think.

How am I different from them?
Now don't go explaining your personalities and the rest of it.

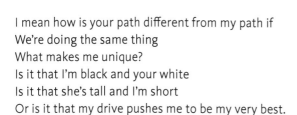

I mean how is your path different from my path if
We're doing the same thing
What makes me unique?
Is it that I'm black and your white
Is it that she's tall and I'm short
Or is it that my drive pushes me to be my very best.

The only thing that keeps me going
Is a desire to do something else.

Maybe you feel the same way,
But maybe you're thinking to yourself
"Whatever I'm good
I'm living my life in the now and its how I want to do it"

But is it wrong to think to the future
is it just accepted to go down some winding paths
to end up where you could've been 6 turns ago if you had listened.
I will say you have to make your own mistakes,
But where is the line?
Where do you cross it?
And what will make your line different from mine?
What makes me unique

118 THE BIRTH OF SUCCESS

Lincoln Heights Book-In- A-Week Program

400 50TH STREET N.E.

WASHINGTON D.C. 20019

Visit by CYITC Program Director Kerrian Peart

Jasmia and Chynna

Lincoln Heights Youth Program last day

Mr. Ingram giving Bullying Poem Lesson

Lincoln Heights Youth make silent poem

122 THE BIRTH OF SUCCESS

BULLYING POEM

Kiamonee Smith

I remember once upon a time my friend was getting bullied
In just one minute he was tortured from someone he knew
They started throwing things at him made him cry too
Listen up bullies it's really unfair
When we beg them to stop they really don't care
It seems the people they bully are the true people they fear
Not from violence but from getting ahead

BULLY ME WHY?

Chynna Dandridge

Why do you hit me and
Make me cry?
Why do you tease me?
Tell me why
You make fun of my family
My clothes and my shoes
And when a crowd comes
Around you're even more amused
You hurt my feelings
And no matter how hard I try, I still cry
So now I'll stand up to you I won't run and
Go proudly I will say I have a 4.0; you know
Just be my friend you could have a chance.

BULLYING POEM

Zyaja Cook

Don't under estimate anyone because
Nothing will be funny.
Go ask your parents for money
When you are knocked out, it won't be like honey
Never run away like a scared little donkey
The bully's day will go from cloudy to sunny
They will make you feel like you have
Butterflies In your tummy.
Bullies just want your $10 bill
The only thing they do for a living is steal
I bet they take anger management pills.

BULLYING POEM

Jonquil Hawkins

Austin Moon belongs on the moon
Austin Moon moves like a balloon
I'm small but I can ball like a small forward
When I cry I can fly like a pie
I'm skinny and funny but like honey
When I talk and walk I feel like a fork
When you bully other people you might feel
Like you go hard but you really a soft dork
Think you are tough and just as rough
Need a cloth to fall when you bully for sport
When you pick or mess with younger people you smile
Bully or saying mean things on the internet dial
That's bullying

BULLYING POEM

Jasmia Hawkins

Please don't sit and laugh at me, don't call me names,
Don't make excuses to gain pleasure from my pain.
They tease little boys with glasses
They always call them a geek,
A little girl who never smiles
Because she have braces on her teeth
Bullied children know how it feels to cry to sleep
I see that kid on every playground
Who's always chosen last
Or the single teenage mother
Tryin' to overcome her past
You don't have to be their friend
But is it too much to ask: Don't laugh at people
Don't call people names
Don't get your pleasure from another people's pain

BULLYING POEM

Cortez Smith

Fist punch.
Foot crunch.
Hand hit.
Mouth spit.
Eye swells.
Can't see.
Please,
Please,
Let me be.

THE BIRTH OF SUCCESS

Rips my homework.
Steals my money.
Grabs my lunch.
Thinks it's funny.

I won't tell, I swear I won't.
Please don't do that. I said, "Don't!"

Sticks and stones may break my bones...
Sissy
Prissy
Four-eyes
Geek
Fatso
Stupid
Nerdy
Freak
...but names can really hurt.

Through the doors.
Up the stairs.
Face is bloody.
No one cares.

In the washroom.
Clean up the mess.
I'll be safe
Until ... recess.

THE BULLY

Alijah Gladden

They all try to look the same
all try to give themselves a name
pick on the boy who is all alone
just because his identity is his own
what has this world come to?
all this wrong that people do
just for the image they want to show
down the evil path they seem to go

The next person you go to hurt
or try to make feel like dirt
instead of trying to look cool
feel for the guy you make look a fool

A cool identity isn't a need
let those you bully be freed
Your identity should be your own
A better person you will be known.

YOU ARE THE HATER

Willis Davon

You are the hater who says I am fat.
You are the hater who knocks off my hat.
You are the hater who laughs at my spots.
You are the hater who pulls on my locks.
You are the hater who causes me grief.
You are the hater who smirks at my teeth.
You are the hater who screws up my work.
You are the hater who calls me a jerk.
You are the hater who will go down for this.
I am the victim who no one will miss.

BULLYING POEM

Taichelle Miller

I'm so upset
I can't go on
I want to die
They made me cry
They called me names
They pulled my clothes
They sprained my wrist
They broke my nose
They followed me home
They tripped me up
They stole my diary
They ripped it up
They really scared me

They made me bleed
One had a knife
One had speed
I didn't tell
I kept it quiet
My lip sliced with wire
I'm sorry, Mom
I'm sorry, Dad
Hope you understand
It was really bad
The hurt was too much
As well as the pain
If it didn't stop
I would have gone insane
I felt trapped
I felt alone
I couldn't cope
I was on my own
I went to bed
I cried all night
Every night the same
Until I died.

BULLYING POEM

Chardonae Zimmerman

They tear you apart,
they get in your head,
they shatter your heart,
they make you feel dead.
They somehow get deep,
way into your mind,
secrets they won't keep,
and more they will find.
They share them with friends,
so people can hear,
your rumor is out,
and so is your fear.
They ruin it all,
your life they could end,
too strong and too tall,
for you to defend.
They punch and they kick,
their words oh so strong,
they are just so sick,
they are just so wrong.
They do have a lot,
and they are really smart,
But they don't have one thing,
and that's a good heart.

132 THE BIRTH OF SUCCESS

WHERE I'M FROM

Jasmia Hawkins

Where I'm from that messy side of town
Where everybody lay down

Where I'm from it's all the clowns
Trying their best to fake frowns

Where I'm from you can't see me
But I see you

Where I'm from we party all day
Until the sun go down

Northeast where they run that town

WHERE I'M FROM

Jovonte Campbell

Where I'm from
We dance all night
Someone step on my shoes
We must fight
Where I'm from
We be loud
It's to sound like we
In a large crowd
I live in Lincoln Heights
Yesterday it was a couple of fights
Lincoln Heights not fun anymore
People always knocking at my door
I love Lincoln Heights
I love it with all my might

WHERE I'M FROM…

By Zyaja Cook

Where I'm from
They say it's the home of the gamecocks.

We might dance all night
When it comes to sport we put you at fright

Where I'm from it's full of fun
The love is in the air dusk to sun

When people drive by
We make them stare

Where I'm from they say
It's a small town but nobody cares

When it comes to having class,
We would get the crown
That's where I'm from
That's how we get down

WHERE I'M FROM

Jonquil Hawkins

Lincoln Heights run their town
Kids play with toys and tag around
If you don't live here, you only wish you could.
I am coolin' on 50th and Banks
But my nickname is tank.
This is my hood

WHERE I'M FROM

Alijah Gladden

Where I'm from people shoot all night
There's never no sleep
Don't let bed bugs bite
Where I'm from people party
All night they always rap but their
Raps are not tight
Where I'm from the police are mean
They come out and everyone has to bounce
Where I'm from people always fight
There is never a night that is fully nice
That where I'm from!!

WHERE I'M FROM POEM

Chynna Dandridge

I am from D.C. Southeast
I am from killings and police sirens at night
I am from late nights outside
I am from little kiddy fights
I am from a great family that's loving and caring
And some are from broken household strong and steady
Don't ever judge me

WHERE I'M FROM POEM

Secret Webb

Where I'm from there is a wide group of people
Some are young and some are old

There are a lot places to go
A lot of mystery to unfold

Where I'm from there is a lot of land
But a place with no sand

Where I'm from is kind of boring
Birds are singing and rain is pouring

Where I'm from people come and go
Even if they say know

Lincoln Heights is on a chill hill
It's really chill

Ugh many people are killed
Lincoln Heights is still very chill

It's in N.E.
Not S.E.

My family lives here
I love them near

haikus
&
clerihews

138 THE BIRTH OF SUCCESS

CLERIHEW POEMS

Jamel Hawkins

Michael Jackson

Was the world's best dancer
He did the moonwalk
Just like a panther

Jay–Z

Was a big fool
He dropped out school
Got a baby by Beyoncé
That ain't cool

CLERIHEW POEM

Shmirah Horton

Jay-Z

Rap like a bee
He can't touch me
He needs to pay baby fee

CLERIHEW POEM

Chyna Ann McLain

Live On Blaine
She Sing like a Crain
And she can't be blamed

CLERIHEW POEM

Secret Webb

Pink

She is my favorite singer
Love her lyrics
Her swag is meaner

CLERIHEW POEM

Chynna Dandridge

Meek Mill

He needs a pill
He don't pay no bills
He lives on a hill

CLERIHEW POEM

Keyon Webb

Lebron James

Game Is Tight
But he thinks he always right
He received a backcourt violation
And still the best in NBA.

CLERIHEW POEMS

Chardonae Zimmerman

Nicki

Is the best female rapper
Always wearing pink and black
Probably work in the Back
Of a donut shack

Lightshow

He makes them know
Songs to go let them go
Words flow gets them girls
Cause that's my Lightshow

CLERIHEW POEMS

Kiamonee Smith

Chris Brown

Look like a clown
Tall look a donkey
And look like a monkey

Jay-Z

He love Mrs. B
That why he had a baby
Name Blue Ivy

CLERIHEW POEMS

By Zyaja Cook

Chief Keef

He belongs at the bottom of the reef
This fool smell like raw beef
So broke, he had to become a thief

Lil Wayne

He gives me pain
His rhymes drive me insane
Nicki Minaj is his main

Jay-Z

Has a baby named Ivy
He is married to Mrs. B
He ugly as heck, can't you see

Chris Brown

Think he needs a crown
He over here looking
Like a clown
He made Rihanna bow down

CLERIHEW POEMS

Alijah Gladden

Lil Wayne was the best
Until he looked like a past
That needs to rest

Meek Mill

Always fail
He needs some bail
He lives in jail

CLERIHEW POEMS

By Jovonte Campbell

Lil Wayne

He the best in the game
One of his raps made the
Crowd go insane

Chris Brown

He is a clown, needs to
Get out of town
Also he is a hash brown

HAIKU COURAGE POEMS

Chynna Dandridge

Bravery is strength
Courage makes splendid amour
Valor keeps our men

Courage to see you
I need courage to hold you
So I do not run

Some use death to flee,
But suicide lacks honor.
Living takes courage

A silver lining
Painted on a dull, gray sky
By courage and faith

A hero never dies
Even when he loses his battle
Courage sustains him

Made in the USA
Charleston, SC
20 October 2014